Unveiling the Enigmatic Beauty of Romania.

TRANSYLVANIA, ROMANIA TRAVEL GUIDE 2024

ETHAN BRISBANE

TABLE OF CONTENTS

CHAPTER 1

INTRODUCTION TO TRANSYLVANIA

Greetings from Transylvania, a land rich in culture, history, and breathtaking scenery! Allow me to take you on a tour of this fascinating country as your informed tour guide, sharing insights about its rich history, varied landscapes, and distinct charm.

1.1 A synopsis of Transylvania

Located in the centre of Romania, Transylvania is well known for its breathtaking scenery, historic villages, and folktales that have captivated people for generations. The Carpathian Mountains, which border this picturesque area to the east and south, provide stunning views and outdoor adventures for those who enjoy the outdoors. The undulating hills, thick forests, and charming villages of Transylvania provide a tranquil setting for travel and exploration.

1.2 Cultural Significance and History:

Transylvania's history is both intricate and fascinating, having been shaped over the ages by influences from many different cultures. There is proof that humans have lived in the area for thousands of years, indicating that it was once inhabited. Transylvania has hosted a wide variety of civilizations throughout its history, with influences from the Roman, Hungarian, Saxon, and Romanian peoples all leaving their marks on the region and its inhabitants.

The tale of Count Dracula, which was based on the real-life Vlad the Impaler, is one of Transylvania's most enduring legacies. Numerous tourists have been drawn to the area by this legendary link, eager to explore the numerous fortified churches and mediaeval castles that dot the terrain. But Transylvania's cultural legacy goes far beyond vampire culture; it includes an intricate web of customs, folklore, and handicrafts that are still practised today.

1.3 Climate and Geography:

The geography of Transylvania is typified by its varied topography, which includes fertile agriculture, undulating plains, and mountain ranges and valleys. A large portion of the terrain is dominated by the Carpathian Mountains, which provide breathtaking views and outdoor activities including hiking, skiing, and wildlife observation. Numerous rivers in the area meander through the countryside, providing water for agriculture and transportation. These include the Târnava, Olt, and Mureș.

Transylvania has a continental climate, meaning there are four distinct seasons. Summers are great for outdoor activities and sightseeing because they are typically warm and sunny. Autumn is a popular season for nature enthusiasts to visit because of the colourful foliage and colder temperatures. Winters can be bitterly cold and covered with snow, especially in the mountainous regions. This makes for great conditions for winter activities and warm evenings by the fireplace. The emergence of blossoms and regrowth in the springtime makes Transylvania's countryside and villages the ideal destination for exploration.

To sum up, Transylvania is a place of unmatched natural beauty and cultural diversity that provides travellers with a unique experience. This charming region of Romania has much to offer everyone, whether they are lured by its colourful customs, breathtaking scenery, or rich history. So gather your belongings, and let's go on an exploration of Dracula's territory and beyond!

CHAPTER 2

PLANNING YOUR TRIP

Greetings and welcome to the planning phase of your Transylvanian adventure! I'm here to assist you manage the many facets of trip planning as your amiable and informed tour guide, ensuring a seamless and unforgettable vacation in this enchanted area. Now let's discuss the key information you should have in mind when organising your trip to Transylvania:

2.1 Best Time to Visit

There are four distinct seasons in Transylvania, and each has its special beauty that draws tourists in. The ideal time to go will mostly rely on your interests and the activities you want to do:

- **Spring (March to May):** Springtime in Transylvania is a great season to enjoy outdoor pursuits like hiking, cycling, and visiting the countryside because of the blossoming flowers, lush vegetation, and cooler temperatures. The weather is usually nice, though erratic with sporadic downpours possible.

- **Summer (June to August):** With pleasant temperatures and extended daylight hours, summer is Transylvania's busiest travel season. It's the perfect time for outdoor activities and sightseeing. During this time, there are many festivals and cultural events that provide tourists an opportunity to fully experience the local way of life. But be ready for more people and more expensive pricing, particularly in well-known tourist locations.

- **Autumn (September to November):** Transylvania's autumn is distinguished by breathtaking beauty as the leaves change colour, producing a charming setting for exploring. It's a perfect time for hiking, wine tasting, and touring historic sites because the weather is still pleasant. In addition, there won't be as many tourists as there are in the summer.

- **Winter (December to February):** With snow-capped mountains, quaint Christmas markets, and chances for winter sports like skiing and snowboarding, winter turns Transylvania into a winter wonderland. Winter can be a lovely season to visit if you love snowy vistas and warm evenings by the fire. However, the lower temperatures may put off other tourists.

The ideal time to travel to Transylvania ultimately relies on your tastes and areas of interest. Everyone can find something to enjoy all year round in this fascinating location, whether they like to spend their time outside on adventures in the summer months or cuddling up by the fire in the winter.

2.2 Visa Requirements :

Make sure your country of citizenship has the necessary visa requirements before you travel to Transylvania. Although Romania is a member of the European Union (EU), it is not a part of the Schengen Area, so depending on your nationality, different visa requirements may be applicable.

- **EU/EEA Nationals:** There is no visa needed for citizens of EU and EEA nations to enter Romania. Within 180 days, they can enter with a valid passport or national ID card for stays of up to 90 days.

- **Citizens of non-EU/EEA countries:** Before visiting Romania, visitors from non-EU/EEA countries may need to obtain a visa. For the most recent information, you must verify with the Romanian embassy or consulate in your country, as the specific criteria differ based on your nationality.

- **Transit Visas:** Depending on your country and the duration of your layover, you could require a transit visa if you're travelling via Romania on your way to another location. To prevent any problems on your travels, make sure to review the requirements for a transit visa well in advance of your departure.

Before leaving for Transylvania, be sure you have all the required visas or travel permits and that your passport is valid for at least six months after your intended stay in Romania. If the standards are not met, admission may be refused or there may be issues at the border.

2.3 Transportation Options:

Transylvania's advanced transportation system makes travelling there and around it reasonably simple. When making travel plans, take into account the following modes of transportation:

- **Air Travel:** Flying into one of the major airports in the region is the most convenient method to get to Transylvania. Cluj-Napoca International Airport (CLJ), which serves both domestic and international flights to locations around Europe, is the biggest in Transylvania. Târgu Mureş Internaţional Airport (TGM) and Sibiu International Airport (SBZ) are two additional airports in the area. To get to your final destination from the airport, you can take public transportation, hire a car, or hail a cab.

- **Train Services:** Transylvania and beyond can be easily explored by train because of Romania's vast railway network. The major cities and towns in the region are connected by regular train services run by the Romanian National Railway Company (CFR Călători). In general, trains are comfortable, reasonably priced, and provide beautiful views of the surrounding area. To guarantee your seat, it is recommended that you purchase your tickets in advance, particularly during periods of high travel demand.

- **Bus Networks:** Another well-liked way to get through Transylvania is by bus, especially to go to the smaller towns and villages that aren't serviced by railroads. Numerous bus companies provide routes that connect the region's main cities and popular tourist spots. Buses can be more expensive and less dependable than trains, but because of their frequent stops along the route, they might take longer to arrive at your destination.

- **Car Rental:** If you want to travel independently and explore off-the-beaten paths or rural locations that are difficult to reach by public transit, renting a car is a practical way to see Transylvania. Transylvania is home to numerous domestic and foreign automobile rental businesses that provide a large selection of cars to fit your demands and price range. Remember that some nationalities may need an International Driving Permit (IDP) to drive in

Romania, so make sure to confirm the requirements before hiring a car.

- **Taxi Services:** Taxis provide a practical means of local transportation and are widely accessible throughout Transylvania's major cities and tourist destinations. To guarantee a reasonable fare, it is best to utilise authorised taxis that are fitted with metres. As an alternative, for increased convenience and transparency, you can use ride-hailing applications like Uber or Bolt.

Regardless of the mode of transportation you select, exploring Transylvania is a pleasant experience that lets you take in the breathtaking landscapes, quaint towns, and lively local culture of this alluring region.

2.4 Accommodation Options:

Transylvania provides a wide variety of lodging choices to fit every preference and price range, including opulent hotels, boutique guesthouses, quaint bed & breakfasts, and rustic farm stays. When you are organising your trip, take into account these well-liked lodging options:

- **Hotels:** Transylvania has a wide range of hotels, from luxurious resorts to low-cost chains, all providing guests with cosy lodging and contemporary conveniences. Major cities and popular tourist spots in the region provide a wide variety of lodging alternatives, whether you're looking for a five-star luxury experience or a small, family-run hotel.

- **Guesthouses and B&Bs:** If you're looking for a more individualised and intimate stay in Transylvania, think about booking a room in a guesthouse or bed and breakfast. These little lodgings, which are frequently owned by neighbourhood families, provide warm rooms, homemade meals, and intimate knowledge of the top local attractions. It's a fantastic way to support small businesses and fully experience the friendliness and culture of the area.

- **Rural Retreats:** If you're looking for a tranquil getaway from the bustle of the city, you might want to book a room in a farmhouse or rural guesthouse in the Transylvanian countryside. These charming homes provide a peaceful, natural environment in which you may unwind, rest, and enjoy classic Romanian hospitality. For a more immersive experience, many rural retreats also provide activities like hiking, horseback riding, and farm visits.

- **Airbnb and homestays:** If you're looking for a more genuine and immersive experience, book a stay with a local host on homestay websites like Airbnb. This gives you the chance to interact with locals, discover more about their way of life, and get exclusive knowledge of Transylvania's customs and culture. Airbnb provides a range of lodging choices to meet your needs, whether you're searching for a solitary room in a nearby house or a complete apartment.

- Camping and glamping are popular options in Transylvania if you're an outdoor enthusiast or just like to spend your nights beneath the sky. The area is home to a large number of glamping and camping locations that provide gorgeous natural settings, contemporary amenities, and chances for outdoor pursuits like stargazing, hiking, and fishing.

Camping and glamping offer a distinctive way to take in Transylvania's natural beauty, whether you wish to set up a tent in the woods or enjoy the opulence of a luxury safari tent.

To discover the ideal spot to stay during your trip, take into account budget, location, and facilities when selecting lodging in Transylvania. Transylvania provides a variety of lodging options to meet the needs of any traveller, whether they are looking for luxury and comfort or authenticity and adventure.

In conclusion, there are several things to take into account while organising a vacation to Transylvania, including the ideal time to go, the necessity for a visa, the available modes of transportation, and the types of lodging. You can guarantee a seamless and pleasurable journey to this alluring area, where adventure is waiting around every corner, by doing your homework and making advance plans. So gather your belongings, get ready for a life-changing adventure, and get ready to discover Transylvania's treasures!

CHAPTER 3

GETTING TO TRANSYLVANIA

Greetings from the next stage of your Transylvanian journey: the journey there! I'm here to provide you with all the information you need to have the most flawless travel experience in this fascinating area as your knowledgeable tour guide. Let's examine the different ways to get to Transylvania by transportation:

3.1 Major Airports and Airlines for Air Travel

The easiest and fastest way to get to Transylvania is usually via plane, as the region is accessible from several major airports. Transylvania is a magical place to visit. The following list includes some of Transylvania's major airports along with the airlines that serve these locations:

- **Cluj-Napoca International Airport (CLJ)** is the biggest airport in Transylvania and a key hub for both local and international flights. It is situated close to the city of Cluj-Napoca. Regular flights are offered by airlines including Ryanair, Tarom, Wizz Air, and Lufthansa to cities in Europe like Munich, Istanbul, London, and Paris.

- **Sibiu International Airport (SBZ):** Located in the city of Sibiu, SBZ connects travellers to several locations throughout Europe via both domestic and international flights. Airlines that fly to cities like Stuttgart, Dortmund, and Vienna include Austrian Airlines, Blue Air, and Wizz Air.

- **Târgu Mureș Internațional Airport (TGM)** is a regional airport that connects to locations in Romania and Europe. It is situated close to Târgu Mureș. There are flights to Budapest, Tel Aviv, and Bucharest from airlines including Wizz Air and TAROM.

- **Other Regional Airports:** Transylvania is home to several smaller regional airports, such as Oradea International Airport (OMR), Satu Mare International Airport (SUJ), and Baia Mare Airport (BAY), which provide a limited number of domestic and international flights, in addition to the major airports previously mentioned.

It's critical to evaluate costs, itineraries, and airline policies while making travel arrangements to select the finest trip to Transylvania. Remember that demand and the time of year might affect flight availability and frequency, so it's best to purchase your tickets well in advance, particularly during the busiest travel times.

3.2 Railroad Services

An easy and beautiful method to see Transylvania and the neighbouring areas is by train. The vast railway network that connects Romania's major cities and towns provides travellers with convenient and reasonably priced modes of transportation. When travelling to Transylvania by train, keep the following points in mind:

- **Principal Train Stations:** Cluj-Napoca, Sibiu, Braşov, Timişoara, and other cities are home to Transylvania's principal train stations. Traveller facilities, waiting lounges, and ticket offices are all well-equipped in these stations.

- **Domestic Routes:** Major cities and towns in Transylvania are connected to other parts of the nation by frequent train services provided by CFR Călători, the national railway company of Romania. There are several classes of trains with differing degrees of comfort and facilities, such as first class (InterRegio) and second class (Regio).

- **International Routes:** Transylvania is connected to neighbouring nations including Hungary, Serbia, and Bulgaria with international train services in addition to local routes. Trains from Timișoara to Belgrade and Cluj-Napoca to Budapest are two well-liked international lines.

- **Reservations and Tickets:** You can buy rail tickets at train stations, online at the CFR Călători website, or via accredited ticket sellers. It's best to purchase your tickets well in advance, particularly for international and long-distance travel, as trains can fill up rapidly, particularly during the busiest travel seasons.

- **Travel Advice:** It's important to get to the station early when taking a train in Transylvania to give yourself enough time to buy a ticket and board. Before getting on the train, make sure you confirm your ticket. If you don't, you could be fined. Keep your possessions safe and pay attention to your surroundings at all times, especially on crowded trains and stations.

3.3 Buses Networks

Buses are a common way of transportation for those looking for cost and flexibility when visiting Transylvania. Numerous bus companies provide quick and comfortable transportation choices for passengers by operating routes that connect major cities and towns in the region. What you should know about travelling to Transylvania using bus networks is as follows:

- **Bus Stations:** Cluj-Napoca, Braşov, Sibiu, Timişoara, and other cities are home to Transylvania's major bus stations. Passenger amenities, waiting areas, and ticket offices are all present in these stations.

- **Domestic Routes:** Several bus companies provide regular routes between Transylvania's major cities and towns and other parts of Romania. There are various types of buses, such as standard and premium, with differing degrees of amenities and comfort.

- **International lines:** Transylvania is connected to other nations including Hungary, Serbia, and Bulgaria with international bus services in addition to local lines. Buses from Cluj-Napoca to Sofia and from Sibiu to Budapest are frequent international routes.

- **Reservations & Ticketing:** Bus tickets can be bought at bus stations, online via the websites of bus operators, or from licensed ticket sellers. Since buses can fill up rapidly, particularly during the busiest travel seasons, it is advised to purchase your tickets in advance, especially for long-distance and international journeys.

- **Travel Advice:** It's important to be at the station early when taking a bus in Transylvania to give yourself enough time to buy a ticket and board.

Make sure the bus driver or conductor can see your identification and ticket when they inspect you. Furthermore, stay aware of your surroundings and secure your possessions, particularly when riding packed buses.

3.4 Driving Tips and Car Rental Options

For those who would rather have the independence and flexibility to see Transylvania at their own pace, renting a car is a great choice. Travelling by automobile enables you to find hidden jewels and off-the-beaten-path locations that might not be easily accessible by public transit, thanks to its well-maintained highways and picturesque driving routes. Here are some vital driving advice for Transylvania, along with several car-rental options:

- **Driving in Transylvania:** Drivers in Romania are required to sit on the left side of the vehicle and adhere to right-hand driving regulations. The usual speed restrictions are 50 km/h in cities, 90 km/h on rural roads and 130 km/h on highways. However, these figures can change based on the particular road conditions and signs. Before you go behind the wheel, make sure you are familiar with the local traffic laws and regulations.

- **Road Conditions:** Although certain rural areas may have narrower or less developed roads, the majority of Transylvania's roadways are well-maintained and safe for driving. Particularly in hilly areas, be ready for sporadic potholes, road construction, and erratic driving conditions.

- **Options for Car Rentals:** There are numerous domestic and foreign car rental businesses operating in Transylvania, and they provide a large selection of cars to fit your demands and budget. Among the well-known automobile rental firms are Hertz, Sixt, Europcar, and Avis. Major airports, train stations, and city locations are the places where you can pick up rental automobiles. One-way rentals and variable rental dates are available.

- **Booking and Insurance:** To guarantee availability and get the best deals, it's imperative to reserve in advance when renting a car in Transylvania, particularly during the busiest vacation seasons.

Make sure you thoroughly review all of the terms and conditions of your rental agreement, especially the ones about insurance coverage, fuel policies, and additional costs. For further driving comfort, think about getting comprehensive insurance.

- **Navigation and Safety:** Make sure to plan your route ahead of time and utilise GPS or navigation software to help you along the way before embarking on your road trip. Keep your passport, driver's licence, and rental agreement close at hand. You should also always abide by the speed limits and traffic laws in your area. Pay attention to your surroundings and drive carefully, especially when you're in an unknown place or bad weather.

In conclusion, there are numerous transportation options to fit every traveller's interests and budget, making it simple and comfortable to reach Transylvania. There are many ways to explore this enchanted area and unearth its hidden gems, whether you decide to fly, ride the train, board a bus, or hire a car. So prepare for an amazing tour through the heart of Transylvania by packing your bags and planning your itinerary!

CHAPTER 4

EXPLORING TRANSYLVANIA

Greetings from Transylvania, a land rich in history, folklore, and breathtaking scenery just waiting to be explored. I'm excited to take you on a tour of some of the most famous locations and activities that this fascinating area has to offer in my capacity as your informed tour guide. Transylvania offers a unique experience with its stunning mountain vistas, historic castles, quaint towns, and cultural attractions. Now take your camera, pack your bags, and let's go exploring!

4.1 Top Destinations

i. Bran Castle
Often referred to as "Dracula's Castle," Bran Castle is one of Transylvania's most well-known sites and a must-see for fans of both vampires and history. Situated on a steep ledge close to Bran town, this formidable stronghold, which dates back to the 14th century, is shrouded in stories and legends.

Discover legends about Vlad the Impaler, royal intrigue, and mediaeval warfare while exploring the  castle's creepy hallways and hidden passageways.

From the castle's towers, enjoy expansive views of the surrounding landscape, and don't forget to take a picture of the recognizable turrets set against the Carpathian Mountains.

ii. Sighişoara Castle

Explore the cobblestone lanes of Sighişoara Citadel, one of Europe's best-preserved mediaeval cities and a UNESCO World Heritage Site, and travel back in time. This walled castle, tucked away in the heart of Transylvania, is a veritable gold mine of historical sites and architectural marvels.

Explore the mediaeval clock tower, which provides breathtaking views of the town below, and pay a visit to

Vlad the Impaler's birthplace, which is housed within the citadel walls.

Get lost in the winding alleyways with their vibrant homes, unique stores, and charming cafes; each turn reveals a different tale from centuries ago.

iii. Peleş Castle

Peleş Castle, a masterpiece of Neo-Renaissance architecture

and a symbol of Romania's royal lineage, is regarded as one of Europe's most magnificent castles. This fanciful castle will captivate your mind. It is situated in the charming village of Sinaia, at the base of the Carpathian Mountains.

Explore the castle's luxurious apartments and chambers and marvel at the opulent interiors with their beautiful wood carvings, stained glass windows, and priceless artwork.

Admire the elaborate fountains, statues, and well-kept lawns that accentuate the castle's majesty and attractiveness as you stroll around the surrounding gardens.

iv. Brasov's Old Town

Brasov Old Town is a blend of mediaeval elegance, Baroque  architecture, and dynamic culture, nestled in the shadow of the Carpathian Mountains. This charming town gives an insight into Transylvania's rich past with its majestic city walls, mediaeval squares, bustling markets, and lively cafes.

Enjoy a stroll around the old town's cobblestone streets, where you can see architectural gems including Catherine's Gate, Council Square, and the Black Church.

Discover the town's undiscovered beauties, such as its enchanting artisan stores, secret passageways, and courtyards, where you can find one-of-a-kind presents and mementos.

v. Highway Transfagarasan

The Transfagarasan Highway connects the provinces of Transylvania and Wallachia by winding through the stunning scenery of the Southern Carpathians. It is widely recognized as one of the most scenic drives in the world.

Constructed as a military route of strategic importance, this engineering masterpiece offers breathtaking vistas and driving sensations as it winds through untainted forests, steep valleys, and craggy mountains.

Take a car journey along the Transfagarasan Highway, which is home to hairpin turns, vertiginous switchbacks, and breathtaking scenery at every corner.

Along the way, make stops at picturesque vistas, alpine lakes, and hiking paths to stretch your legs, take pictures, and take in the Carpathian Mountains' unspoiled splendour.

4.2 Outside Activities

i. Hiking In the Carpathian Mountains

There are countless options for outdoor adventure and discovery in the Carpathian Mountains because of its large wilderness regions, rocky peaks, and picturesque paths. There is a hiking path in Transylvania to fit every interest and skill level, whether you are an experienced hiker or just a casual

nature enthusiast. Hike through Piatra Craiului National Park's lush forests and alpine meadows to see breathtaking scenery, a variety of fauna, and expansive vistas of the surrounding mountains.

Take on a challenging climb up Romania's highest mountain, Moldoveanu mountain, which is situated in the Fagaras Mountains. You'll cross glacier lakes, rocky terrain, and snow-capped summits en route, all of which will lead to a satisfying sense of success at the summit.

ii. Observing Wildlife

Transylvania is a wildlife and nature lover's dream come true because of its abundance of diverse flora and fauna. Some of the most recognizable animals in Europe find refuge in the region's national parks and protected areas, including wolves, chamois, and brown bears.

Explore the isolated forests and meadows of the Apuseni Mountains with a guided wildlife excursion in search of elusive animals like European bison, wild boar, and golden eagles.

Visit the Libearty Bear Sanctuary, located close to Zarnesti, where rescued bears live freely in roomy enclosures. Here, you can get up close and personal with these magnificent animals and discover the work being done to preserve Romania's natural heritage.

iii. Cycling Routes

Transylvania provides a network of beautiful roads and trails that meander through quaint towns, breathtaking scenery, and significant historical sites for those who enjoy bicycling. Transylvania offers a variety of cycling experiences, from exhilarating mountain descents to peaceful rides along country lanes.

On the Transylvanian Wine Route, bike past historic wineries, ancient fortifications, and picturesque rural landscapes as you explore the undulating hills and vineyards of Tarnava Mare.

Try your mettle on the Apuseni Mountains' paths, which provide steep terrain, difficult climbs, and exhilarating descents. This picturesque area offers a variety of mountain riding experiences, from singletrack paths to woodland trails.

4.3 Cultural Encounters

i. Customary Celebrations

People from Transylvania come together to celebrate traditional music, food, and customs during lively festivals and rich cultural traditions. The vibrant parades, ethnic dances, handicrafts, and delectable food offered during these festivals provide a singular window into the history and culture of the area.

Savour the enchantment of the Sibiu International Theatre Festival, one of Europe's most prestigious performing arts gatherings, when international theatre companies come to Sibiu to display their skills on outdoor stages and historic settings.

Experience the joy at the centuries-old Brasov Junii Parade, which happens the first Sunday following Easter. Riders dressed in traditional garb ride through Brasov's streets in honour of the city's patron saints and to bless the local population.

ii. Local Cuisine and Dining

A trip to Transylvania wouldn't be complete without sampling some of the delectable food, which combines Saxon, Romanian, and Hungarian influences. Every taste is catered to in Transylvania, where delectable pastries, exquisite cheeses, and robust stews, and grilled meats await.

Savour classic Romanian food mainstays like mămăligă (polenta served with sour cream and cheese), sarmale (cabbage rolls loaded with meat and rice), and ciorbă de perişoare (meatball soup).

Discover real street food delicacies like covrigi (pretzels), langos (fried dough covered with cheese and sour cream), and kürtőskalács (chimney cake) by visiting the local markets and food booths in cities and villages throughout Transylvania.

iii. Artisan Workshops and Markets

Transylvania is well known for its extensive history of artisanal skills and workmanship, with craftsmen and artisans continuing ancient customs that have been passed down through the years. Transylvania's artistic legacy is exhibited through the distinctive and exquisite creations made by the region's artists, which range from weaving and embroidery to woodcarving and pottery.

Visit artisan workshops and studios in locations like Sibiu, Cluj-Napoca, and Miercurea Ciuc to witness the labour of talented artisans and buy handcrafted trinkets, presents, and souvenirs to bring back home.
Discover the year-round local markets and craft festivals, which provide an abundance of locally made foods and drinks along with traditional handicrafts, textiles, ceramics, and folk art.

In summary
Transylvania is a region of limitless possibilities, where there is always something new to discover around every corner—whether it is a secret treasure or an intriguing tale just begging to be shared. With its recognizable castles, mediaeval villages, unspoiled environment, and lively cultural scene, this enchanted area has enough to offer every kind of traveller. Therefore, Transylvania encourages you to go out on a journey of discovery and wonder, whether your interests lie in the region's rich culinary and cultural

traditions, its natural beauty and outdoor adventures, or its history and folklore. You won't regret visiting Transylvania to discover its magic for yourself!

CHAPTER 5

FREQUENTLY ASKED QUESTIONS (FAQs) ABOUT TRAVELLING IN TRANSYLVANIA

You probably have some concerns about what to expect, how to keep safe, and how to deal with local customs as you get ready to travel to Transylvania. Do not be alarmed! To make sure you have a hassle-free and delightful time touring this fascinating area, I'm here to provide you with the answers to some of the most frequently asked concerns.

Q1. Is it safe to travel across Transylvania?

Visiting Transylvania is usually a safe idea. Just as anywhere else, you should use common sense and take safety steps to make sure you're safe. Transylvania is not known for violent crime, however pickpocketing and small-time larceny are common, particularly in popular tourist locations. Keep your possessions safe, pay attention to your surroundings, and avoid going for a nighttime stroll by yourself in strange places if you want to stay safe. Furthermore, it's a good idea to familiarise yourself with any potential safety risks or travel advisories before your trip, as well as to observe all applicable local rules and regulations while in Transylvania.

Q2. What is the official currency of Transylvania?

The Romanian Leu (RON) is the official currency of Romania, which includes Transylvania. Banknotes are available in quantities of 1, 5, 10, 50, 100, and 200 lei, while coins are available in denominations of 1, 5, 10, and 50 bani. The leu is known as the "RON" and is divisible into smaller units called "bani." It is a good idea to have some cash on hand for minor purchases and transactions, especially when travelling to rural areas or visiting local markets and vendors, even if major credit and debit cards are accepted at hotels, restaurants, and larger businesses in tourist areas. Obtaining Romanian Lei during your visit is simple because banks, exchange offices, and ATMs all around Transylvania offer currency exchange services.

Q3. Are people in Transylvania generally English-speaking?

In Transylvania, English is commonly spoken, particularly among younger generations, in major cities, and tourist areas. Although Romanian is the official language, many people, especially those in the tourism sector, speak German, Hungarian, or French in addition to English, which they may speak quite well. To converse with locals, it's beneficial to learn a few simple words in Romanian or utilise a translation tool, as there might be fewer English speakers in more isolated or rural locations. Generally speaking, you should have no problem getting by in Transylvania with English; but, learning a few words of the native tongue is usually appreciated and can enrich your cultural experience.

Q4. What attire is appropriate for visiting places of worship?

It is important to respect local customs and religious traditions by dressing modestly and respectfully when visiting holy places in Transylvania. This usually refers to protecting your knees, chest, and shoulders and avoiding exposing apparel like shorts, tank tops, and low-cut shirts for both men and women. In addition, it's traditional to show respect by taking off your hat and sunglasses when visiting monasteries or cathedrals. While some religious locations may supply visitors who are not dressed suitably in scarves or covers, it is best to arrive prepared with modest clothing that honours the holiness of the location you are visiting. By wearing appropriately, you promote a courteous and good cross-cultural interchange while demonstrating respect for the local community's religious traditions and beliefs.

Q5. Which common practices and manners are there?

To ensure a seamless and pleasurable stay, travellers should be aware of Transylvania's, as well as the rest of Romania, unique customs, traditions, and social etiquette. The following customary practices and manners to bear in mind when visiting Transylvania are listed:

- **Greeting Etiquette:** It is polite to extend a strong handshake and make eye contact when you are meeting someone for the first time. Perhaps a small head nod or bow might also be appropriate in more formal situations or while interacting with elderly people. Unless you are invited to use their first name, address people using titles like "domn" (Mr.) or "doamnă" (Mrs.) followed by their last name.

- **Transylvanian eating customs:** It is courteous to wait for the host or hostess to extend an invitation before settling in at the table. It's also traditional to wait to start eating until the host or the oldest person has finished. You should also keep your hands above the table during the meal. If your host insists on giving you extra food or seconds, don't be shocked; this is a gesture of kindness and hospitality.

- **Elder Respect:** Elder respect is highly esteemed in Romanian society, and older people are expected to be addressed with courtesy and civility. When conversing with an individual who is older than you, use formal language and demonstrate your respect by standing when they enter the room and giving them priority when it comes to food or seating arrangements.

- **Gift Giving:** As a sign of gratitude, it's common to provide a modest gift for your host when you visit their home or attend a social event. Appropriate gifts are chocolates, champagne, or flowers. Make sure you give the gift with both hands and let them know how much you appreciate their hospitality.

- **Personal Space:** Although Romanians are generally kind and amiable, they also respect one another's personal space and could stand closer to one another during talks than you might be used to. Respect people's boundaries and be aware of this cultural difference, particularly when engaging with strangers or in busy public areas.

Understanding these typical etiquette and practices will improve your interactions with locals throughout your travels in Transylvania, in addition to demonstrating respect for their culture and traditions. Never forget that wherever you go, a little decency and thoughtfulness go a long way toward building meaningful connections and unforgettable experiences.

In summary

I hope this book has helped you with some of the questions you may have had regarding safety, money, language, customs, and manners as you set off on your trip to Transylvania. You'll be better able to negotiate the cultural quirks of this unique location and have an unforgettable and fulfilling travel experience if you are aware of and respectful of the customs and traditions of the locals. So prepare for an exciting journey of exploration and discovery right in the heart of Transylvania by packing your baggage and keeping an open mind!

CHAPTER 6

UPDATED 2024 INFORMATION

What's New in Transylvania?

There are a ton of thrilling updates, events, and attractions waiting for you when you travel to Transylvania in 2024. Transylvania never fails to enthral tourists with its breathtaking scenery, fascinating history, and friendly people. From colourful festivals and cultural events to increased security and brand-new attractions, the region has plenty to offer everyone. Let's explore the most recent information and upgrades to make sure you have a magical time discovering this area.

6.1 Festivals and Current Events

Transylvania is a hive of activity in 2024, with a schedule jam-packed with thrilling festivals and events that highlight the region's rich cultural legacy. Whatever your interests—music lovers, foodies, or history buffs—Transylvania has something to offer everyone. Here are a few of the most notable occasions and celebrations for 2024:

- **Sighişoara Medieval Festival:** Every year, the UNESCO World Heritage-listed town of Sighişoara hosts the Sighişoara Medieval Festival, which transports visitors back in time and lets them experience the enchantment of the Middle Ages. Visitors may immerse themselves in the mediaeval past of the area with this multi-day event, which includes costumed parades, mediaeval reenactments, traditional music and dance performances, artisan markets, and more.

- One of the biggest and most prominent film festivals in Eastern Europe is the Transylvanian Film Festival (TIFF), which movie buffs won't want to miss. TIFF, which takes place in Cluj-Napoca, features a wide range of foreign and Romanian cinematic works, including experimental, short, and feature films. The festival is a must-attend event for both industry professionals and movie buffs because it offers workshops, panel discussions, and special events in addition to film screenings.

- The annual Halloween celebration at Bran Castle, sometimes referred to as "Dracula's Castle," is held on October 31st. If you're looking for a creepy and unique Halloween experience, don't miss it. Travellers from all over the world go to this historic festival to reveal beneath the shadow of the fabled fortification. Savour live performances, costume competitions, themed activities, and, of course, the opportunity to explore the castle's enigmatic hallways and hidden passageways after dark.

- **Transylvania Wine Festival:** Come celebrate the region's growing wine industry with a glass of wine at the Transylvania Wine Festival, where you may taste a variety of regional wines, including native varieties like Fetească Neagră and Fetească Albă. This yearly celebration of Transylvania's winemaking tradition includes wine tastings, vineyard excursions, culinary workshops, and cultural performances. It takes place at several places around the region.

These are but a handful of the numerous celebrations and events that Transylvania will host in 2024. To make the most of your time in the area, make sure to check local event calendars and websites for the most recent details on dates, venues, and ticket availability. Then, plan your vacation appropriately.

6.2 Safety Updates

Transylvania has made visitor safety and well-being a primary concern, and to improve visitor safety in 2024, the area has put in place several policies and initiatives. Transylvania is dedicated to giving all visitors a safe and delightful experience, from enhanced infrastructure and transportation networks to heightened security measures and health protocols. The following important safety updates should be noted:

- **Improved Transportation Infrastructure:** To increase connection and accessibility for travellers, Transylvania has made investments to upgrade its roads, trains, and airports. It is now simpler to travel within the region and to nearby locations thanks to major road initiatives like the construction of new transportation hubs and the rehabilitation and extension of highways.

- **Increased Security:** To protect tourists, Transylvania has increased security at major tourist destinations, transit hubs, and public areas in response to international security concerns. To stop and address possible threats, this entails stepped-up surveillance, a conspicuous security presence, and coordination with law authorities.

- **Health and Safety Procedures:** Transylvania has put in place health and safety procedures to shield tourists and locals from the virus's propagation in light of the ongoing COVID-19 epidemic. This includes vaccination and testing requirements for certain activities and places, social distancing measures, enhanced cleaning and sanitization procedures, and mask-wearing restrictions in indoor public spaces. During their visit to Transylvania, visitors are kindly asked to follow these rules and stay up to date on any revisions or modifications to public health regulations.

- **Emergency Services and Support:** Transylvania offers a strong network of emergency services and support mechanisms to help visitors in the event of an emergency or unanticipated situation. For tourists in need, this includes having access to medical facilities, emergency response teams, language help services, and information hotlines.

Transylvania is dedicated to providing a secure and inviting environment for visitors, even if travelling always has inherent hazards. These safety updates and actions are intended to ensure a positive and memorable experience for all travellers.

6.3 New Attractions or Services

Transylvania is home to several brand-new services and attractions that, in addition to the thrilling events and safety enhancements, provide tourists with exceptional experiences and chances to explore the area in 2024. Transylvania offers new and interesting discoveries for anybody interested in history, outdoor activities, or cultural immersion. Here are some highlights of the area's newest offerings in terms of services and attractions:

- **Transylvanian Railway Adventure:** The recently launched Transylvanian Railway Adventure takes passengers on a picturesque train ride through the centre of Transylvania. Through breathtaking scenery, quaint towns, and well-known sites, this immersive experience takes passengers on a historic rail line that offers jaw-dropping vistas and life-changing experiences. For a distinctive and unforgettable way to see Transylvania by rail, select from a range of themed excursions and picturesque itineraries, including steam train rides, wine-sampling tours, and heritage railway adventures.

- **Eco-Friendly Accommodations:** By introducing eco-friendly lodging options and eco-resorts that emphasise environmental preservation and responsible travel, Transylvania is adopting sustainable tourism practices. Stay in boutique hotels, guesthouses, and eco-friendly lodges that employ renewable energy sources, and locally sourced products, and reduce waste and carbon emissions. Enjoy peaceful, immersive stays in Transylvania's unspoiled natural surroundings while participating in ecotourism activities like nature hikes, wildlife spotting excursions, and courses on organic farming. You can also support conservation efforts by doing these things.

- **Experiences in the Kitchen:** Treat your taste buds to the newest culinary adventures and gastronomic treats in Transylvania, where a rising number of eateries, cafés, and food tours provide guests with the opportunity to enjoy farm-to-table meals, creative culinary creations, and traditional Romanian cuisine. Discover the secrets of Transylvanian cuisine from local chefs and craftsmen by enrolling in cooking classes and culinary workshops. You can also experience the specialties and delicacies of the region by visiting food markets, festivals, and street food vendors.

- **Adventure Tourism:** Transylvania offers a variety of adventure tourism activities and heart-pounding experiences to satisfy the needs of outdoor enthusiasts and adrenaline seekers. Transylvania offers an abundance of thrilling activities, like zip-lining, rock climbing, white-water rafting, and paragliding, among its mountainous landscapes and natural playgrounds. Take part in outdoor expeditions and guided adventure trips with knowledgeable instructors and guides, and push yourself with thrilling activities that highlight the finest of Transylvania's wilderness and outdoor experiences.

These are only a handful of the brand-new experiences and amenities that Transylvania has in store for you in 2024. Transylvania never fails to enchant visitors with its timeless charm and limitless opportunities for exploration and discovery. It is known for its rich history, breathtaking landscapes, and kind people. Transylvania offers a plethora of novel and captivating experiences for both novice and experienced travellers alike. Come discover for yourself what makes this region so unique!

In summary

I hope this guide has given you useful information and insights into the most recent changes, events, and attractions in the area as you get ready for your trip to Transylvania in 2024. Transylvania has an abundance of chances for exploration, adventure, and cultural immersion, ranging from lively festivals and improved security to novel experiences and amenities. So prepare for an amazing tour through the heart of Transylvania by packing your baggage and keeping an open mind!

CHAPTER 7

ITINERARY SUGGESTIONS FOR EXPLORING TRANSYLVANIA

Are you prepared to travel through the heart of Transylvania on an amazing adventure? This charming area has a plethora of adventures just waiting to be discovered, whether you have a weekend, a week, or longer to spare. Transylvania offers adventure, history, and scenic beauty at every turn, with everything from ancient castles and quaint towns to spectacular landscapes and cultural riches. Let's look at some suggested itineraries to help you get the most out of your trip to Transylvania.

7.1 Weekend Getaway: Two Days of Highlights

A weekend trip is the ideal way to take in most of Transylvania if you're pressed for time but still want to see the main attractions. This is a suggested two-day adventure schedule:

i. First Day:

Morning:

- One of Transylvania's most recognizable sites, Bran Castle, sometimes referred to as "Dracula's Castle," is a great place to start the day. Discover the interesting history and stories of the castle, explore its mediaeval chambers, and climb its turrets for sweeping views of the surrounding landscape.

- After touring the castle, go to the quaint town of Braşov, where you can peruse the booths at the bustling Council Square market, stroll through the Old Town, and take in the Gothic-style Black Church.

In the afternoon:

- Savour typical Romanian dishes like mămăligă (polenta), grilled meats, and sarmale (cabbage rolls) at a leisurely meal at a nearby restaurant.

- After a leisurely drive through the lovely village of Râşnov in the afternoon, you can see the mediaeval Râşnov Citadel. Discover the fortress's past as a defensive bastion, take in the expansive views of the surrounding mountains, and explore the premises.

Evening:

- After supper, head back to Braşov to see the lively nightlife of the town, which includes hip clubs, live music venues, and comfortable cafes.

ii. Day 2:

Morning:

- Visit the quaint village of Sighişoara first thing in the morning. Known for its cobblestone alleys and well-maintained mediaeval architecture, Sighişoara is a UNESCO World Heritage Site. Discover the town's historical core, ascend the recognizable Clock Tower for sweeping views, and pay a visit to Vlad the Impaler's birthplace.
- Visit the neighbouring village of Viscri, which has a wonderfully preserved fortified church and classic Saxon homes, after touring Sighişoara. After learning about the church's significance and history on a guided tour, stroll through the town and enjoy the peaceful rural ambiance.

In the afternoon:

- Savour a typical Romanian lunch in a guesthouse or taverna in Viscri, where you may sample dishes prepared from scratch using ingredients that are found locally.
- Enjoy a leisurely drive through the Tarnava Mare region's undulating hills and vineyards in the afternoon, with a stop at a nearby winery for a sample of Transylvanian wines. Discover how wine is made, taste a variety of varietals, and take in the breathtaking views of the surrounding landscape.

Evening:
- After a full day of seeing, head back to your Brașov or Sighișoara lodging to rest and recuperate. After treating yourself to a delectable supper at a neighbourhood eatery, spend the evening lounging at your hotel or taking strolls across the town.

7.2 A Weeklong Journey: Seeing Several Cities

A week spent seeing different cities and areas of Transylvania would provide a deeper look at the country. This is a possible seven-day adventure schedule:

Day 1: Getting to know Cluj-Napoca
- Upon reaching Cluj-Napoca, the biggest city in Transylvania, delve into its cultural scene, historic sites, and bustling eateries throughout the day.

Day 2: Sibiu to Cluj-Napoca
- Enjoy a beautiful journey from Cluj-Napoca to Sibiu, including a stop at the renowned salt mine and charming village of Turda along the way.
- Explore Sibiu's Old Town, with its cobblestone streets, baroque churches, and mediaeval squares, in the afternoon. Don't miss the magnificent Brukenthal Palace or the well-known Bridge of Lies.

Day 3: Brasov to Sibiu
- Leave Sibiu and head to Brasov, making stops along the road to see the UNESCO-listed town of Viscri and the fortified church at Biertan.

- After arriving, spend the afternoon touring Brasov's old defences, colourful architecture, and quaint cafes in the Old Town.

Day 4: Rasnov Fortress and Bran Castle
- Visit the neighbouring fortifications of Rasnov and Bran Castle, popularly known as "Dracula's Castle," on a day excursion from Brasov.
- Discover the enigmatic rooms and turrets of Bran Castle before ascending to the summit of Rasnov Fortress to get sweeping views of the surrounding landscape.

Day 5: Sighișoara to Brașov
- Leave Brasov and make your way to Sighisoara, making stops along the way to see the mediaeval town of Rupea and the fortified church at Prejmer.
- Explore the old town of Sighisoara in the afternoon, taking in the vibrant homes, cobblestone streets, and mediaeval towers. Don't miss Vlad the Impaler's birthplace and the famous Clock Tower.

Day 6: Cluj-Napoca to Sighişoara

- Return to Cluj-Napoca after leaving Sighişoara, making a stop at the town of Viscri and its exquisitely restored fortified church.
- After touring Cluj-Napoca's parks, gardens, and cultural attractions during the day, have supper at one of the best restaurants in the city as a farewell.

Day 7: Leaving

- Leave Cluj-Napoca for your next destination, carrying with you the memories of a week spent discovering the best parts of Transylvania.

7.3 Off the Beaten Path: Hidden Gems and Rural Experiences

Transylvania has a lot of undiscovered treasures and rural adventures for tourists looking for a more unique travel experience. Here's a suggested plan for seeing some of the lesser-known locations in Transylvania:

Day 1: Getting to Sibiu

- After arriving in Sibiu, a quaint mediaeval city renowned for its well-maintained ancient centre, spend the day touring its mediaeval fortifications, baroque churches, and cobblestone streets.

Day 2: Alba Iulia to Sibiu

- Leave Sibiu and head to Alba Iulia, which has a wealth of ancient sites and one of Romania's most striking fortifications.
- Explore Alba Iulia's fortress complex, with its formidable walls, colossal gates, and opulent cathedrals, throughout the day. The magnificent Union Hall and the exquisitely restored Roman Catholic Cathedral are not to be missed.

Day 3: Hunedoara to Alba Iulia

- Leave Alba Iulia and proceed to Hunedoara, the location of one of Europe's most magnificent mediaeval castles, the fabled Corvin Castle.
- Explore Corvin Castle's great halls, secret corridors, and towering turrets all day long as you discover more about its intriguing past and folklore.

Day 4: Sighisoara to Hunedoara

- Leave Hunedoara and proceed to Sighişoara, a town recognized as a UNESCO World Heritage Site for its charming cobblestone alleys and intact mediaeval architecture.

- Take a day trip to Sighisoara's ancient centre, where you may climb the famous Clock Tower and see Vlad the Impaler's birthplace.

Day 5: Biertan to Sighişoara

- Leave Sighisoara and head to Biertan, a quaint village renowned for its ancient Saxon architecture and fortified church that is on the UNESCO World Heritage List.
- Take a day to explore the mediaeval alleyways and old church complex of Biertan, while soaking up the peaceful rural atmosphere.

Day 6: Viscri to Biertan

- Leave Biertan and head to Viscri, a charming village renowned for its traditional way of life and exquisitely maintained fortified church.

- Explore Viscri's old church complex, meet local craftsmen and artisans, and dine at a guesthouse serving traditional Romanian cuisine.

Day 7: Leaving

- Take with your recollections an unforgettable and immersive rural adventure deep within Transylvania as you depart Viscri for your next destination.

There is a wonderful itinerary waiting for you in Transylvania, no matter how much time you have available. Transylvania provides countless opportunities for exploration, discovery, and adventure, whether you're looking for a weekend escape, a week-long trip, or something off the beaten road. Prepare for an incredible tour across this captivating region by packing your baggage and putting on your hiking boots. It's Transylvania time!

CHAPTER 8

LANGUAGE AND COMMONLY USED PHRASES IN TRANSYLVANIA

Immersion in the local culture is one of the pleasures of visiting a new place, and language acquisition is crucial to that experience. The Romanian language is spoken in Transylvania, a historical and culturally rich region; yet, you will also come across distinctive dialects and idioms that showcase the region's varied background. Knowing a few basic words and being aware of the local dialects can improve your trip and help you connect with the people you meet along the route, whether you're ordering food at a local restaurant or striking up a discussion with a friendly local. Let's explore the interesting world of Transylvanian dialects and expressions by delving into some key phrases.

8.1 Essential Romanian Expressions for Visitors

Even though most people in Transylvania speak English in tourist areas and larger cities, trying to learn a few words of Romanian can help you connect with locals and demonstrate your respect for their culture. To aid you in navigating Transylvania throughout your travels, here are a few fundamental Romanian phrases:

i. Hello/Goodbye:

- **English:** Hello/Goodbye
- **Romanian:** Buna ziua/Buna dimineata (Hello) / La revedere (Goodbye)

ii. Please/Thank you:

- **English:** Please/Thank you:
- **Romanian:** Te rog/Mulțumesc

iii. Yes/No:

- **English:** Yes/No
- **Romanian:** Da/Nu

iv. Excuse me/Sorry:

- **English:** Excuse me/Sorry
- **Romanian:** Scuzați-mă/Îmi pare rău

v. Do you speak English?:

- **English:** Do you speak English?
- **Romanian:** Vorbiți engleză?

vi. I don't understand:

- **English:** I don't understand
- **Romanian:** Nu înțeleg

vii. Where is...?:

- **English:** Where is...?
- **Romanian:** Unde este...?

viii. How much is this?:

- **English:** How much is this?
- **Romanian:** Cât costă acesta?

ix. Can I have the check, please?:

- **English:** Can I have the check, please?
- **Romanian:** Pot să am nota, vă rog?

x. Cheers!:

- **English:** Cheers!
- **Romanian:** Noroc!

When utilising these phrases, keep in mind to talk clearly and slowly. If necessary, don't be hesitant to gesture or make simple hand signals to help explain what you mean. Even if your Romanian is not very good, most people will still appreciate your effort to communicate in their language, and it can result in some remarkable conversations and cross-cultural exchanges while you are visiting Transylvania.

8.2 Transylvanian Dialects and Expressions

Transylvania is home to several distinctive dialects and phrases that, in addition to standard Romanian, reflect the region's rich cultural legacy. The linguistic environment of Transylvania is rich and diverse, ranging from traditional Romani and Saxon communities to influences from Germany and Hungary. The following are some examples of dialects and idioms you could hear in Transylvania:

i. Hungary Influence :

- Hungarian terms and idioms are frequently employed with Romanian in everyday conversation because of the historical presence of Hungarian communities in Transylvania, especially in locations with sizable Hungarian populations. For instance, "Köszönöm" (gratitude) and "Igen" (yes) are frequently heard in Hungarian-populated towns and villages.

ii. German Influence:

- German vocabulary and expressions are still in common usage in Transylvania thanks to the influence of the Saxon community. For instance, in regions with a significant Saxon population, one may hear the phrases "Guten Tag" (Good day) and "Auf Wiedersehen" (Goodbye).

iii. Romani Influence:

With a long history in Transylvania, the Romani people—also called Gypsies—have had a variety of cultural and linguistic influences on the regional languages. In casual situations and among Romani populations, one may encounter Romani phrases and idioms, which give Transylvania's linguistic fabric a bright and lively touch.

iv. Regional Dialects:

You will also come across regional expressions and dialects in Transylvania that differ from village to hamlet and town to town. These dialects represent the regional traditions and customs of each community and can differ from standard Romanian in vocabulary, pronunciation, and grammar.

Even a rudimentary familiarity with standard Romanian can help you connect with individuals you meet and navigate your travels, even though mastering the subtleties of Transylvanian dialects and expressions may take some time and absorption in the local culture. Thus, embrace the linguistic diversity of Transylvania, and don't be afraid to use your language skills—after all, it's all part of the trip!

To fully immerse yourself in the rich cultural fabric of this fascinating country, you need to become conversant in basic Romanian words and learn about the dialects and idioms used in Transylvania. So gather your phrasebook, polish your language abilities, and get set to go through the heart of Transylvania through language!

CHAPTER 9

ADDITIONAL RESOURCES FOR YOUR TRANSYLVANIA ADVENTURE

It's critical to have access to the appropriate information while you get ready for your trip to Transylvania to improve your travel experience and guarantee a hassle-free and joyful trip. There are many tools available to assist you in organising and navigating your journey across this fascinating region, ranging from travel apps and websites to suggested reading and contact details for embassies and tourism offices. Let's look at a few more tools you can utilise to get the most out of your visit to Transylvania.

9.1 Websites and Travel Apps

Transylvania travel planning and organisation is made easier with the abundance of travel applications and websites accessible in today's digital age. These tools may simplify your travel experience and offer helpful information and insights along the way, from organising lodging and transportation to learning about local attractions and locating the finest places to dine. The following websites and apps are suggested for your Transylvanian adventure:

i. Booking.com: A well-known website for lodging reservations, Booking.com has a large selection of lodging choices, including hotels, guesthouses, flats, and bed & breakfasts. It's simple to locate the ideal location to stay in Transylvania with Booking.com's customer reviews, maps, and search criteria.

ii. Google Maps: An indispensable navigation tool, Google Maps lets you easily navigate Transylvania with its comprehensive maps, driving directions, and real-time traffic information. Google Maps is a useful tool for exploring the area since it can be used to find neighbouring points of interest, eateries, and attractions.

iii. Rome2rio: This all-inclusive trip planner assists you in identifying the most cost-effective ways to get from one place in Transylvania to another. Rome2rio offers route maps, schedules, and pricing information to help you plan your trip and evaluate various travel alternatives, whether you're travelling by train, bus, car, or aeroplane.

iv. <u>XE Currency Converter</u>: This useful tool lets you calculate exchange rates and convert currencies while you're on the road. You may quickly convert the Romanian Lei to your local money and plan your travel budget while visiting Transylvania with the help of up-to-date exchange rate information.

These are only a handful of the several websites and travel apps that can assist you in organising and arranging your trip to Transylvania. Don't be afraid to utilise technology to enhance and de-stress your travel experience. Just be sure to look into additional tools and resources that meet your unique needs and preferences.

9.3 Suggested Reading

There are many books and other materials available for travellers who want to learn more about Transylvania's history, culture, and tourist sites. These can help you gain a deeper understanding and appreciation of the area. These suggested books offer insightful analyses of Transylvania's rich past, regardless of your interest in Dracula, mediaeval history, or modern Romanian culture. You might want to add the following books to your list of things to read:

i. Bram Stoker's classic novel "Dracula": No discussion of Transylvania would be complete without mentioning Bram Stoker's iconic work "Dracula." Its story of the legendary vampire Count Dracula and his encounters with the valiant Englishman Jonathan Harker has captivated readers for generations. For everyone interested in learning more about the most well-known legend from Transylvania, "Dracula" is a must-read, regardless of their preference for horror or historical fiction.

ii. "Transylvania: History and Reality" by Ioan-Aurel Pop: This rigorous yet approachable examination of the region's intricate past and present provides a thorough summary of Transylvania's history, culture, and identity. This book, written by eminent Romanian historian Ioan-Aurel Pop, offers insights into the rich ethnic and cultural legacy of Transylvania, from its mediaeval beginnings to its contemporary significance in Romania.

iii. "Sighişoara: Birthplace of Vlad Dracula" by Catalin Grigore: This intriguing examination of the mediaeval town of Sighisoara and its relationship to the notorious ruler provides a deeper dive into the history and tales surrounding Vlad the Impaler. This book, written by local historian Catalin Grigore, explores the historical details and folklore surrounding Vlad's life and legacy, offering an engrossing look into the sinister and enigmatic history of Transylvania.

iv. William Blacker's "Traditional Romanian Village Communities: The Transition from the Communal to the Capitalist Mode of Production in the Danube Region" provides a thorough ethnographic analysis of village life and agricultural practices in Transylvania for readers interested in rural life and traditional culture. This book, written by anthropologist William Blacker, offers a nuanced perspective on Transylvania's rural history by shedding light on the social, economic, and cultural dynamics of Romanian village communities.

9.4 Embassies and Tourism Office Contact Details

It's crucial to have access to trustworthy information and support when travelling in Transylvania in case of crises or unforeseen circumstances. In case of any medical emergency, lost passports, or assistance with visa matters, the following contact details for embassies and tourism offices can be of great use to you while you're travelling:

i. Embassies and Consulates: It's a good idea to become acquainted with the contact details of your nation's embassy or consulate in Romania if you're visiting Transylvania from abroad. Consular representatives can help with emergency medical care, emergency passport replacement, legal matters, and other consular services. Make sure you have the contact details for the embassy or consulate with you when you travel.

ii. Romanian National Tourist Office: If you need help or information organising your trip to Romania, especially Transylvania, the Romanian National Tourist Office is the place to go. The tourist office can offer helpful tips and ideas to help you make the most of your time in Transylvania, whether you need information on lodging, transportation, attractions, or events. For assistance with travel-related questions, get in touch with the Romanian National Tourist Office via phone, email, or the official website.

iii. Local Tourism Offices: Maps, brochures, and information on local services, hotels, and attractions can be obtained at local tourism offices or information centres in many of the Transylvanian cities and towns, in addition to the national tourist office. These tourism offices are manned by experienced individuals who can offer tailored advice and support to help you organise your schedule and maximise your time in Transylvania.

You may improve your trip and make the most of your time discovering the fascinating area of Transylvania by making use of these extra resources. These tools, which range from travel applications and suggested reading lists to embassy contacts and tourism offices, provide helpful advice, information, and support to enable you to plan and execute your trip with ease and confidence. Prepare for an incredible journey in Transylvania by packing your bags and downloading your preferred travel apps!

CHAPTER 10

FINAL THOUGHTS

Exploring the Enchanting Land of Transylvania

It's time to take stock of the memories you've created, the experiences you've shared, and the adventures that have occurred during your travels through this fascinating region as your voyage through Transylvania draws to an end. Transylvania has mesmerised tourists with its rich history, varied culture, and stunning scenery for centuries. From mediaeval castles and quaint towns to rough mountains and verdant forests, the region has much to offer. Let's review a few last suggestions, advice, and words of wisdom as you get ready to say goodbye to Transylvania so you can cherish your memories of this magical place.

10.1 Final Tips and Recommendations

- **Accept the Unexpected:** Embracing the unexpected and going with the flow is one of the pleasures of travelling. Be open to new experiences and let Transylvania surprise and excite you at every turn, whether it's discovering a hidden gem, getting to know a friendly local, or trying a new meal.

- **Respect the Environment:** Keep in mind to step lightly and leave no mark while you discover Transylvania's natural beauties. To help protect the area's natural landscapes for the enjoyment of future generations, respect the native flora and animals, stick to authorised pathways, and dispose of rubbish correctly.

- **Support Local Communities:** To help the region's economy and cultural legacy, take into account supporting local businesses and artisans when dining, shopping, and making travel arrangements in Transylvania. Your support has a significant impact on the communities you visit, whether you choose to dine at a family-run restaurant or purchase handmade items from a local market.

- **Maintain Flexibility:** While it's important to plan your vacations ahead of time and have a basic agenda, don't be scared to stray from your schedule and enjoy some spontaneity when you go. Adapting to new circumstances, such as extending your stay to attend a local festival or rerouting your itinerary to see a new community, can lead to unforgettable experiences and surprising discoveries.

- Remember to Take Pictures, Journal Entries, or Sketches to Preserve Memories of Your Time in Transylvania. These experiences, whether it's a breathtaking sunset over the Carpathian Mountains or a bustling street scene in a mediaeval town, will be treasured keepsakes of your trip through this fantastical country.

- **Remain Alert and Informed:** Although Transylvania is a relatively safe place for tourists to visit, it's important to remain aware of local laws, customs, and safety precautions. Keep an eye on your surroundings, take security measures for your valuables, and heed any advice or suggestions from tourism or municipal authorities.

10.2 With love, goodbye Transylvania

As your time in Transylvania comes to an end, pause to cherish the moments you've spent and the experiences you've had in this wonderful place. Transylvania has made a lasting impression on your heart and spirit, whether you've been trekking in virgin forests and tasting local food or touring historic castles and mediaeval towns.

Remember that Transylvania's allure will linger with you long after you've left and gone back home. Your life will continue to be inspired and enhanced by the tales you've gathered, the connections you've made, and the breathtaking sights you've seen, serving as constant reminders of the wonders of discovery and the transformational power of travel.

Who knows? Your trip through Transylvania may be only the start of a lifetime of exploration and discoveries that are still to come. Whether you decide to revisit Transylvania to discover more of its undiscovered beauties or explore new places abroad, I hope your travels are full of excitement, wonder, and limitless opportunities.

Thus, as you bid Transylvania farewell, take its essence with you wherever you go, and never forget that the enchantment of this wonderful region will always be there to greet you with open arms upon your return. Until we cross paths again, my traveller, may your travels be full of excitement and may Transylvania's marvels always captivate your heart. Goodbye and have a safe journey!

Printed in Great Britain
by Amazon

38182342R00046